Asking the Right Questions about ADHD

Before, During, and After Your Child's

Diagnosis

Norrine Russell, Ph.D
Heidi Condrey, M.Ed

1st Edition, 2022

Dedication

To Ethan and Lila,

The two of you inspired me to not only create a flourishing coaching practice and write a book to support all of the parents out there struggling with the same questions I once did, but gave me the courage to become a happy mom who loves life.

Ethan, you taught me to love.

Lila, you taught me about joy.

Thank you both.

To Pete,

For always supporting me in every way possible, personally and professionally. I truly couldn't have done this without you.

Thank you for everything.

Praise for the Book

Asking the Right Questions about ADHD Before, During, and After Your Child's Diagnosis

"As a practicing pediatrician and mother of a son with ADHD, I'm deeply aware of and concerned about the challenges we confront with both diagnosing and treating this multifaceted disorder. Dr. Russell's years of experience with ADHD coupled with her passion to educate families provides exactly the support families need to navigate this world. Her evidence-based approach in addressing the behavioral domains of ADHD provides an avenue to empower both the child and the family. Providing children with the skills to harness higher levels of executive functioning to mitigate ADHD will reach far beyond childhood and adolescence. Dr. Russell's proven cognitive approach will equip our children to reach higher levels of success in all areas of life as her methodology can easily translate far beyond the classroom and into sports, relationships and professionalism. I have personally experienced the impact of Dr.

Russell's work. Her book offers the opportunity to help so many others!"

Allison Hull, DO
Dual Board Certified Adult Internist and
Pediatrician

"Dr. Russell brings to bear her extensive knowledge from years of experience working with children with ADHD and their families-- this book provides an accessible window into that vast knowledge putting practical tools into the hands of parents."

Demian Obregon, MD
Psychiatrist
Assistant Professor University of South Florida
Owner Tampa Bay Psychiatry
Owner NeuroSpa TMS

"As a pediatrician who treats ADHD and a mom of a son with ADHD, this is an invaluable resource for families of children with ADHD. ADHD is a complicated diagnosis that encompasses much more than just inattention and hyperactivity. There are lots of other subtleties that are involved in problems with executive function. When the right combination of medication, parent coaching and executive function coaching for the child is used, children *with ADHD can live a normal functional life with the added flares and bonuses that ADHD can bring. Dr. Russell was the executive function coach for my son in the 6th-12th grades. She was an invaluable resource to my son and me. Whereas middle school was chaotic with forgotten papers, low grades due to assignments not turned in, cluelessness about when to start or turn in projects, my son successfully and independently completed his first semester at a university away from home successfully. I am very thankful to have found Dr. Russell and her knowledge she shares in this book will help parents be the best advocate for their child, which is what our children with the diagnosis of ADHD need most."*

Deborah M Gage, MD, MBA
Board Certified Pediatrician

"Just like any neurodiversity, ADHD is a challenge, but there are ways to make the most of it. Dr. Russell does a great job in this book of helping parents with specific challenges, while reminding them that THERE IS HOPE!"

Penn & Kim Holderness
The Holderness Family Podcast

"When I received an ADHD diagnosis with one of my kids I had so many questions and had no

idea what to do. No one seemed to have answers to all of my questions and I know I'm not alone in this. After working with hundreds of parents I am incredibly grateful that Dr. Russell wrote this much needed book for me to recommend to parents. Finally there is a comprehensive resource to answer all your questions, cut through all the confusion and calmly guide parents every step of the way to best support their ADHD kid. Thank you Dr. Russell!"

Sheryl Gould
Parent Educator/Founder of Moms of Tweens and Teens

Introduction

The term ADHD (Attention Deficit Hyperactivity Disorder) can bring up a range of emotions for parents. Sometimes being told that test results indicate, "Your child has ADHD" can bring a sigh of relief and sense of closure to the stage of unknowing. Other times, hearing that same diagnosis results in an onslaught of anxiety, guilt, uncertainty and fear. No matter what specific emotions arise for each family, the next thoughts are usually "What does this mean?" and "What happens next?" Both of those questions are valid and have answers that are complex.

To answer the "what does this mean" question, we must begin to understand what ADHD is, what it is not, how it impacts neurology and consequently how it impacts one's thoughts, abilities and behaviors. We must also know where to look for reliable and valid sources of ADHD knowledge rather than falling prey to the plethora of "junk" information available.

To answer the "what happens next" question, we must understand what resources are available, what treatment options are recommended and how to access both. We must have guidance from ADHD educated professionals who deeply understand ADHD. Fortunately, the American Academy of Pediatrics (AAP) has the following article, *Clinical Practice Guideline for the Diagnosis, Evaluation, and Treatment of Attention-Deficit/Hyperactivity Disorder in Children and Adolescents,* to give us a starting point. From there, we can access numerous informational resources from the AAP. We can seek out the resources of professionals trained in ADHD care and treatment and rely on scientific, evidence-based best practices.

We have created **Asking the Right Questions about ADHD Before, During, and After Your Child's Diagnosis** to provide parents with a definitive, easy-to-digest guide that will function as a tool of empowerment to help you know what questions to ask the professionals. As you dive into this resource and read through the sections, you will find that they detail both the knowledge and tools you will need to navigate your journey with ADHD. The sections of this guide are divided to address the time before the ADHD diagnosis, during the diagnosis and after the diagnosis. Over the years, we have found that knowing the right questions to ask is a tremendous help to parents and that's why we've written this book.

Whatever emotions bubbled up for you when the possibility of an ADHD diagnosis first entered your life, all parents need support navigating the sometimes overwhelming and sometimes conflicting information available. This guide will do just that. So, take a deep breath, sit back and start reading.

Note to Reader

We have written this book to provide parents and others with valuable questions to ask their child's team of professionals. That is our goal--to help you know what questions to ask. Nothing in this book should be construed as professional advice for your child.

Please use this book as a guide to ask the right questions for your child to their teachers, doctors, therapists, and other team members.

Also, we have provided "Looking for more Information?" for each question. These citations are both our references for the information we provide as well as deeper information for parents who want more information.

Contents

Section One: Asking The Right Questions *Before* The Diagnosis

Section Two: Asking the Right Questions *During* The Diagnosis

Section Three: Asking the Right Questions *After* The Diagnosis

Section One

Asking The Right Questions

Before

The Diagnosis

1. What is ADHD?

Attention Deficit Hyperactivity Disorder (ADHD) is a neurological or neurodevelopmental disorder that impacts specific regions of the brain related to planning, focusing and task initiation. Brain chemicals, called neurotransmitters, don't work the same in children with ADHD as they do with neurotypical children. In general, ADHD creates attention difficulties, impulsivity and hyperactivity.

ADHD is the most commonly occurring neurological disorder among children. Some children do outgrow their ADHD symptoms. However, ADHD symptoms can last throughout adulthood making ADHD a common adult diagnosis as well.

Looking for more information?

https://www.cdc.gov/ncbddd/adhd/facts.html

2. When should I get my child evaluated for ADHD?

As the parent, you know your child better than anyone else. Inside and out. Sometimes as parents, we can easily see areas where our children struggle. Other times, we are so filled with hope for who we want our child to be, that we miss important signals happening in front of us. The general guideline is if you are concerned, or a teacher is concerned, it's best to get an evaluation. Think about the following questions as you decide:

Does your child appear to be (as compared to siblings, classmates, teammates, etc.) more talkative, impulsive, and/or active?

Does your child appear to have (as compared to siblings, classmates, teammates, etc.) more trouble following directions or listening?

The AAP guidelines for diagnosis and evaluation of ADHD recommend that primary care providers:

Evaluate children and adolescents

ages 4 to 18 years for ADHD if they are having academic or behavioral problems and show inattention, hyperactivity, or impulsivity.

Sometimes parents do not become fully aware of symptoms until they begin significantly impacting their child at home, childcare or school. If you are able to answer yes to the indicators above, it is time to consider getting your child evaluated for ADHD.

Looking for more information?

https://publications.aap.org/pediatrics/article/144/4/e20192528/81590/Clinical-Practice-Guideline-for-the-Diagnosis?autologincheck=redirected

3. Who should I take my child to for an evaluation?

First, it's important to understand that there are many specialists who can diagnose ADHD. These include pediatricians, neurologists, psychiatrists and psychologists. With so many specialists to choose from, it can be hard to know which specialist is the right one to seek for your child.

So, how do you decide? In order to make that decision, there are a number of factors to consider. The first factor to consider is does your child have simple or complex ADHD? Simple ADHD is when your child shows symptoms of ADHD alone.

Complex ADHD, on the other hand, is when your child has not only the symptoms of ADHD but also the symptoms of other disorders such as depression, anxiety or conduct disorders. If your child is one of the small percentage of children who exhibit ADHD symptoms alone, then you can simply begin with your pediatrician. If your pediatrician is not willing to diagnose your child's ADHD, they will refer you to another licensed professional they recommended to do so.

What if your child has complex ADHD? Then what? At this point it is time to consider what other conditions/disorders your child may have in order to make the best choice for where to seek a diagnosis. If your child is already diagnosed with a neurological condition or you have a family history of seizures or other neurological conditions, a neurologist would be the best place to seek your child's diagnosis. However, if you are more concerned about your child's level of anxiety, depression or other psychiatric issues, a psychiatrist is a more logical place to start.

Another starting point for many families is their child's school. While the school cannot provide a diagnosis, they can complete a psychoeducational evaluation. A psychoeducational evaluation is a complete evaluation of the child both cognitively and emotionally. The results of the psychoeducational evaluation can be used by the school to determine if the child meets the eligibility criteria for special services. To qualify, the child must meet the criteria of one or more of the 13 categories of the IDEA (Individuals with Disabilities Education Act) categories under which students can receive special services. In addition to determining if the student qualifies for special services, the psychoeducational evaluation results will also be used to determine accommodations for the student. Finally, the psychoeducational evaluation results can identify concerns about attention, concentration and memory. These results can then be shared with the professional who is providing the diagnosis for your child.

There are a few things to keep in mind when it comes to working with public schools. First, even though a public (traditional, magnet and charter) school *should* refer your child for an internal evaluation if you or your child's teacher has concerns, that doesn't always mean your child's school *will* refer your child for an internal evaluation. This is especially true at the middle and high school level. You must always be prepared to advocate for your child. If you request an evaluation, the public school is legally obligated under IDEA to evaluate your child for cognitive (including attentional) functioning deficiencies, academic deficiencies, psychological health as well as speech and language deficiencies. If your child qualifies under one or more of the 13 categories, your child may be eligible for an IEP (Individualized Education Program) and/or 504 (accommodation plan). If your child attends private school, the IDEA laws and protections do not apply. Your child's private school may or may not recommend an outside evaluation to you, even if they see your student is struggling. Again, you must be prepared to advocate for your child and seek resources outside of the school.

If your child's school does suggest a referral for internal evaluation, it is important to realize the school has your child's best interests in mind and are genuinely seeking the best ways to understand and offer services to your child. If you are not comfortable with the school conducting the evaluation, you can always opt to have the evaluation done privately by an evaluator of your choice.

What is important is that you act on the concerns being expressed by the school. Fully understanding what is happening is in your child's best interests.

As you start to think about evaluations and a diagnosis, are you beginning to get concerned about the impacts of labeling your child? If so, take a deep breath and realize this is a perfectly normal worry. Then, consider the "labeling" situation from a more logical standpoint. Consider that children who do not have a 504 plan or an IEP still get labeled. However, the label is much more likely to be "lazy" or "troublemaker".

Now that we've unpacked the feeling of anxiety centered around labeling your child, let's look at the crux when it comes to schools. Public or private. Schools may or may not alert you when there is a need for further evaluation for your child. Schools may or may not confirm there is a problem when you raise concerns about your child. You are your child's number one advocate. If you have concerns, it is best to err on the side of caution by having an evaluation completed; either through the school or privately.

Looking for more information?

https://chadd.org/about-adhd/professionals-who-diagnose-and-treat-adhd/

4. Should I wait or should I get an evaluation?

Many parents may intentionally or unintentionally delay getting their child evaluated. Often, the inclination to delay seeking an evaluation is entangled in a knot of fear. Fear of acknowledging something may not be functioning properly within your child, fear your child might not be normal, fear that you may have failed your child, fear this issue with your child may be your fault, fear your child may have a difficult road, fear you may not be strong enough to help your child, fear you may be inadequately equipped to handle this, fear of the stigma of labeling your child, fear of medicating your child, fear of other people's opinions about what may or may not be applicable to your child and how you should handle the concerns with your child, fear of over or under reacting to whatever is causing the concerns with your child... Obviously, we could go on for pages capturing the various fear thoughts that hold parents back from seeking an evaluation for their child. The bottom line is fear is a huge part of our parenting journey. It has been from day one and will continue to be. The sooner you can accept this, the sooner you can move towards solutions.

Once you have accepted fear as a normal reaction to concerns with your child, you can start to tackle this situation from a more logical perspective. If your child had symptoms of diabetes or vision problems, would you be delaying an evaluation? Of course not! If your child broke their wrist playing baseball or experienced a concussion during football, would you delay medical treatment? Of course not! Delaying treatment results in negative consequences that include anything from further injury to irreversible damage.

Signs and symptoms of ADHD should be given the same attention and consideration we would give to any other illness or injury. If your child does have ADHD, it's not going away. If it's not ADHD, you need to know what is causing the difficulty. Either way, by seeking the evaluation you are getting the information you need to move forward.

Looking for more information?

https://publications.aap.org/pediatrics/arti
cle/144/4/e20192528/81590/Clinical-
Practice-Guideline-for-the-
Diagnosis?autologincheck=redirected

5. Does a diagnosis mean my child needs medication?

A diagnosis means the child will do best with treatment. You will work with your clinician to determine the best course of treatment for your child. Although there is no one-size-fits-all approach, research demonstrates that multimodal therapy, which includes medication, is what is most beneficial and overall helpful to the child.

MULTIMODAL TREATMENT IS BEST FOR ADHD

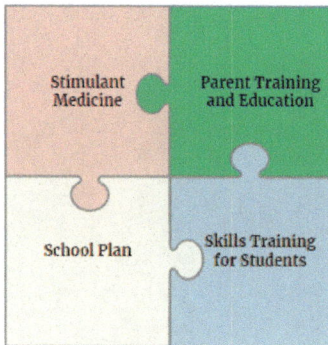

The above graphic helps demonstrate how medication is one piece of the multimodal treatment puzzle. Each piece of the puzzle contributes to your child's treatment plan and works in conjunction with the other pieces. While medication may be a *part* of your child's treatment plan, it should not be the whole treatment plan.

Looking for more information?

https://publications.aap.org/pediatrics/article/144/4/e20192528/81590/Clinical-Practice-Guideline-for-the-Diagnosis?autologincheck=redirected

Section One Summary

We encourage you to take these questions and bring them to conversations with members of your child's team, including their doctor, teacher, school counselor, etc.

Questions to ask BEFORE the diagnosis:

1. What is ADHD?

2. When should I get my child evaluated for ADHD?

3. Who should I take my children to for an evaluation?

4. Should I wait or should I get an evaluation?

5. Does a diagnosis mean my child needs an evaluation?

Remember, your child's best advocate is you! Do not rely on school to tell you if there is a problem. Take these questions to initiate deeper conversations regarding your child. Do not be afraid to ask as many questions as you would like and to continue asking for clarification until you truly understand the next steps and when to move to the evaluation stage. Diagnosing ADHD is complicated so the more you understand, the more likely you will be to make good decisions during this exploratory stage.

If you are not sure how to start this conversation with your child's professionals, please feel free to reach out to Russell Coaching so we can support you.

Section Two

Asking The Right Questions

During

The Diagnosis

1. How will the professional diagnose ADHD?

One important thing to understand is that the ADHD evaluation will come from the lens of the professional perspective of whomever is completing the evaluation. If you recall, an ADHD diagnosis can come from a pediatrician, neurologist, psychiatrist or psychologist. Although each professional will reference either the standard guidelines from the American Academy of Pediatrics (AAP) or the American Psychiatric Association's Diagnostic and Statistical Manual of Mental Disorders (DSM) to make an ADHD diagnosis, each professional will be looking through the "lens" of their specialty area. Each specialist will be concerned with symptoms related to their discipline. This means that a psychiatrist will be concerned about the mental health component of ADHD. A neurologist will be concerned with symptoms such as epilepsy, interrupting sleep cycles and other cerebral impacts. A psychologist will be concerned with symptoms related to behavioral challenges, learning difficulties and anxiety. A pediatrician will have a much more general lens and will be concerned with overall symptoms adversely impacting your child.

Whichever lens the professional uses, they will be using standard guidelines to make the official diagnosis. Depending on the professional you see and your child's particular symptoms, you may need to seek treatment from more than one professional. It will be important to consider which specialty area, specialist lens and expertise is most appropriate for the symptoms your child displays.

Looking for more information?

https://www.cdc.gov/ncbddd/adhd/diagnosis.html

2. How likely is it that my child will be identified as having ADHD if they really don't have it?

Many people worry about a false positive because the ADHD evaluation can seem so subjective. However, other possible reasons for your child's symptoms must be ruled out and your child must meet a threshold to be given an ADHD diagnosis. It is very unlikely that a psychologist, neurologist, or psychiatrist, after completing a thorough exam or evaluation, will give your child a false positive diagnosis. Does it happen? Yes, but rarely. Yes, everyone can be a little inattentive but not everyone is a little ADHD. It is true that the symptoms of ADHD can overlap with many other conditions. However, this is also true for numerous other physical and mental conditions.

Your child will not be diagnosed with ADHD easily or quickly. Conducting a thorough ADHD evaluation is a multi-step process. Your clinician will thoroughly evaluate your child against accepted diagnostic criteria to make an informed diagnostic decision. Evaluations should include scales such as the Conners Rating Scale, the Child Behavior Checklist, the Strengths and Difficulties Checklist, and the ADHD Rating Scale. In addition, your clinician should rule out any alternative explanations for your child's symptoms as part of their overall evaluation. This should include taking a detailed medical history and screening for related conditions. It is also important to remember the high probability of comorbidity with your child's ADHD diagnosis. Comorbid conditions can often create confusion for parents as in these cases the ADHD diagnosis is not the only diagnosis needed.

Looking for more information?

https://www.additudemag.com/diagnosing-adhd-is-difficult/

3. Does my child have simple or complex ADHD? How will I know?

This is an important piece of the puzzle, as two-thirds of kids who receive an ADHD diagnosis also receive a related diagnosis. Complex ADHD is now understood to be the norm, rather than the exception. 60% of children diagnosed with ADHD have at least one comorbid condition. Comorbid, or coexisting, conditions are a separate diagnosis and will require separate treatment. Common comorbid diagnoses include, but are not limited to, specific learning disabilities, anxiety disorders, depression, conduct disorders, mood disorders and autism.

If your child is diagnosed with a related condition in addition to their ADHD diagnosis, your child is considered to have complex ADHD. However, it is important to understand that ADHD is often the first disorder to appear so many times the comorbid conditions may not appear until after the initial ADHD diagnosis. Your child may possibly start out with a diagnosis of simple ADHD and then move to a complex ADHD diagnosis after related conditions appear and are diagnosed.

As the parent, you are your child's most important advocate. You cannot simply rely on the medical professional to automatically consider comorbid conditions. You must ask the medical professional, "Do you think anything else is also at play?" "How do you know?" "What should I watch for?" If they are able to do so themselves, the clinician should assess for comorbid conditions or refer you to the appropriate subspecialist who can do so.

Looking for more information?

https://www.additudemag.com/adhd-in-children-symptoms-comorbidities/

4. Are there other conditions that are likely to coexist with ADHD that I should be aware of and monitoring for?

The first key piece of information needed to understand the relationship between ADHD and coexisting conditions is that any condition can coexist with ADHD. However, there are certain conditions or disorders that tend to coexist more commonly with ADHD. The most common coexisting conditions include behavior disorders such as Oppositional Defiant Disorder (ODD) and Conduct Disorder (CD), mood disorders such as depression, anxiety and bipolar disorder, tics and Tourette Syndrome, learning disorders such as dyslexia, dyscalculia, dysgraphia and speech problems, sensory processing disorder and sleep disorders.

While the possibilities of coexisting conditions may seem a bit overwhelming, being aware and proactive are key strategies to managing whatever challenges your child may face. Once the symptoms that led to the ADHD diagnosis in the first place have improved through the use of a multimodal treatment plan, observe if challenges still persist for your child. If your child is still experiencing challenges at home or at school, even after an ADHD diagnosis and treatment plan, this is a clue that coexisting conditions may be present. Ongoing challenges could include continued learning difficulties despite increased attention, extreme defiance, extreme mood shifts, ongoing anxiety, sleep disturbances and over or underwhelmed responses to sensory stimuli. Another clue indicating a possible comorbid condition is that the symptoms beyond those associated with your child's ADHD diagnosis are both chronic and pervasive. If you notice other symptoms persist once your child's ADHD symptoms are under control, it is time to seek a clinical evaluation to determine if your child is experiencing a coexisting condition.

Looking for more information?

https://chadd.org/about-adhd/co-occuring-conditions/

5. What is ADD and how does it relate to ADHD?

Many people are familiar with the term ADD or Attention Deficit Disorder. For many years, ADD was a commonly accepted term that described someone who experienced the inattentive form of ADHD. This term was used to describe people who struggled with inattention but not necessarily hyperactivity. However, this term is no longer used or accepted in the medical field. Now, the DSM-5 recognizes three types of ADHD. These include predominantly inattentive type of ADHD, predominantly hyperactive-impulsive type of ADHD and the combined type of ADHD. ADD is an outdated term that is no longer used.

Looking for more information?

https://www.webmd.com/add-adhd/childhood-adhd/add-vs-adhd

6. What is the difference between a school evaluation and an outside evaluation?

The most crucial difference to understand regarding school evaluations compared to an outside evaluation is that your child's school cannot diagnose your child with ADHD. However, under the Individuals with Disabilities Education Act (IDEA), your child's school is required to evaluate how your child is experiencing challenges at school and why they might be experiencing those challenges. The comprehensive evaluation conducted through the school will include an assessment in several areas that could include health, vision, hearing, social and emotional health, intelligence, communication, academics and motor skills. The evaluation is intended to be comprehensive enough to identify any and all of a child's special education needs.

In general, the evaluation will be conducted by the school psychologist. However, if necessary, the evaluators can also include therapists such as speech/language, occupational or physical therapists in order to ensure a multidisciplinary approach. The psychoeducational evaluation conducted by the school can indicate concerns with attention, memory and concentration, which could be indicators of ADHD. Since ADHD is not defined by IDEA, your child's school will refer you to an outside provider to make the actual ADHD diagnosis.

A private evaluation can determine if your child qualifies for an ADHD diagnosis. With a private evaluation, you are free to seek out the services of a qualified evaluator of your choice. A private evaluator is not bound by the school district regulations and policies; therefore, a private evaluator can conduct a more comprehensive and deeper evaluation of your child. Your child's evaluator will determine if your child meets the specific diagnostic criteria for an ADHD diagnosis. The evaluator can also make recommendations that can be implemented in the school setting to help your child be more successful.

Looking for more information?

https://www.understood.org/en/articles/private-vs-school-evaluations-pros-and-cons

https://youriepsource.com/school-versus-private-psychoeducational-evaluations/2020/6/22/school-versus-private-psychoeducational-evaluations-things-to-consider-when-making-your-decision

7. What process can I expect in a school evaluation?

Before understanding the school evaluation process, it is necessary to understand what schools are required to do, what they cannot do and what they can do. The Individuals with Disabilities Education Act (IDEA) and Section 504 (of the Rehabilitation Act of 1973) are the primary federal laws that govern the rights of all students (K–12) with disabilities. IDEA requires that all students displaying concerns that impact their school performance are given an evaluation to understand how and why a student is struggling before accommodations or services are offered. The school evaluation will determine whether your child meets one of the thirteen educational classifications, defined by IDEA, and demonstrates an educational need.

The first step in the school evaluation process will consist of written consent. The school cannot evaluate your child without your written consent. Once they have received this consent, the school will then request information from you regarding your child's behavior, strengths and challenges at home as well as at school. Your child's teacher will also be asked to share information regarding your child's academic performance, behaviors, attention issues and any other challenges in the classroom. You will also receive a form to be completed by your child's medical doctor.

Once all of this information has been collected, the school will then begin a formal evaluation of your child. Typically, this consists of the school psychologist conducting standardized assessments with your child. The school evaluation will include analyzing how your child functions in the school environment in general as well as specific aspects of that functioning such as executive functioning, cognitive functioning, communication, behavior and academic skills. If the psychoeducational evaluation indicates concerns with attention, memory and concentration, your child's school will most likely recommend that you seek a private provider to determine if your child's symptoms can be attributed to ADHD.

Looking for more information?

https://chadd.org/for-parents/requesting-an-evaluation-in-public-schools/

https://www2.ed.gov/about/offices/list/ocr/docs/dcl-know-rights-201607-504.pdf

https://www.understood.org/en/articles/the-evaluation-process-what-to-expect

8. What process can I expect in a private evaluation?

If you choose to seek a private evaluation for your child, you do have the option to pursue the evaluator of your choice. As we mentioned earlier, various qualified professionals such as medical doctors, psychiatrists, neurologists, and psychologists can conduct the evaluation. While each professional will ultimately reference either the standard guidelines from the American Academy of Pediatrics (AAP) or the American Psychiatric Association's Diagnostic and Statistical Manual of Mental Disorders (DSM) to determine whether or not your child qualifies for an ADHD diagnosis, the specific steps and rating tools used may vary.

Whatever evaluator you choose, you can expect some combination of interviews, rating scales, and questionnaires about health information, behaviors, strengths, weaknesses and academic information. Once the evaluation is complete, you will most likely have a follow up meeting where you will get the results of the evaluation, the determination for your child and a discussion about treatment if your child has received a diagnosis.

Looking for more information?

https://www.understood.org/en/articles/outside-evaluations-the-difference-between-private-and-independent

https://afsa.org/parents-guide-psychoeducational-evaluations#:~:text=Often%20evaluators%20will%20inquire%20about,your%20child's%20strengths%20and%20weaknesses

9. What is an IEP and does my child need one?

An Individualized Education Plan (IEP) is a written, legal document that outlines the supports and services a child with identified disabilities will receive at school. A child with an ADHD diagnosis alone will most likely not qualify for disability services under IDEA. To be eligible for an IEP outlining special education services, a child must meet one of the thirteen educational classifications defined by IDEA and demonstrate an educational need. In extreme cases, an ADHD diagnosis can fall under the IDEA classification of "other health impairment." However, a child diagnosed with simple ADHD most often does not qualify for an IEP unless their ADHD is so severe it is causing a major impairment. If your child has complex ADHD or other challenges such as a learning disability, they may be eligible for an IEP.

If your child is found eligible for an IEP, the school evaluation team will work with you to determine specific supports, services and goals to be outlined in your child's IEP. You must provide consent for the IEP to be put into place. Your child's classroom teacher is obligated to incorporate any supports, services, accommodations and goals into your child's general education plan. Your child may also receive specialized support from a special education teacher. Your child's IEP plan will be reviewed annually and updated accordingly.

Looking for more information?

https://www.understood.org/en/articles/what-is-an-iep

https://kidshealth.org/en/parents/iep.html

10. What is a 504 plan and does my child need one? What supports does a 504 plan provide?

If your child has an ADHD diagnosis alone that is impacting their learning and results in needing extra support at school, they are much more likely to qualify for a 504 plan than an IEP. A 504 plan falls under Section 504 of the Rehabilitation Act which seeks to ensure the needs of children with physical and mental impairments are identified and addressed the same as they would be for children with disabilities.

Like an IEP, a 504 Plan is a legal, written document. However, the 504 plan will be specific to accommodations and modifications your child will receive and will not include goals or transitional services. A 504 plan can allow for things such as extended test time, quiet testing locations, advanced notice of upcoming tests, specific classroom seating, seating modifications, attention cues from the teacher, fidgets, movement breaks and other accommodations to help your child be successful. Essentially, a 504 plan levels the playing field for your child.

As with an IEP, if your child is found eligible for a 504 Plan, the school evaluation team will work with you to determine specific accommodations to be outlined in your child's 504 Plan. You must provide consent for the 504 Plan to be put into place. Your child's classroom teacher is obligated to incorporate any accommodations into your child's general education plan. Unlike an IEP, a 504 Plan does not require annual review. Instead, a 504 Plan requires periodic re-evaluation, which is generally accepted to be every three years.

Looking for more information?

https://www.understood.org/en/articles/what-is-a-504-plan

https://kidshealth.org/en/parents/504-plans.html

11. Is ADHD considered a learning disability?

Both ADHD and learning disabilities are considered neurodevelopmental disorders. ADHD in and of itself, is not considered a learning disability. However, ADHD is often associated with learning disabilities because it does create difficulties with learning. If you recall from the previous section on coexisting conditions, a learning disability is often a comorbid condition with ADHD. In fact, researchers estimate about 50% of children with ADHD also have a learning disability.

A learning disability can impact specific learning areas such as your child's learning abilities with skills such as reading, writing and math. ADHD, on the other hand, will have a much more general impact affecting areas such as attention, impulsivity and hyperactivity. It is for these reasons that most children with only ADHD may not qualify for an IEP. If they are found eligible, it is usually under "Other Health Impairment" (OHI).

Looking for more information?

https://www.verywellmind.com/is-adhd-a-learning-disability-4116126

https://ldaamerica.org/disabilities/adhd/

https://www.additudemag.com/half-of-all-kids-with-adhd-have-a-learning-disability-or-related-condition/

12. What is executive function and how does it relate to ADHD?

We can think of executive function skills as a set of cognitive managerial skills. Our executive function skills are what allow us to regulate our thoughts, feelings, behaviors and actions.

Thanks to executive function skills we can create and follow through with plans, organize our thoughts and spaces, set and achieve goals on a timeline, self-evaluate, make decisions, and regulate our emotions. Without this set of cognitive skills, we would have difficulties regulating our emotions, initiating or completing tasks, maintaining and shifting focus, retaining information to complete a task, or remembering details.

A person with an ADHD diagnosis often has challenges in the areas of executive function such as creating and following through with plans, setting and achieving goals, regulating emotions and impulsivity, remembering details, organizing materials and spaces, time management and following through with tasks.

It's important to realize that many of the symptoms of ADHD are indicators of missing or weak executive function skills. Individuals with ADHD are not lazy, unmotivated, or just restless; they are simply experiencing weakness in the brain's self-management system.

Looking for more information?

https://www.understood.org/en/articles/what-is-executive-function

https://developingchild.harvard.edu/science/key-concepts/executive-function/

https://www.understood.org/en/articles/difference-between-executive-functioning-issues-and-adhd

13. If my child is prescribed medication, what can I expect?

The most important concept to understand regarding medication is that finding the right medication and dose for your child is a process. We call this process titration and titration is a normal part of the medication process. The goal of titration is to find the most effective medication, dose, and duration for your child that has the least amount of side effects. The prescribing doctor will start your child on a low dose of medication and then slowly raise the dose until your child gets the most benefits with the least amount of side effects. The entire process will take several weeks at minimum.

Once your child has begun taking medicine, you will be the primary person responsible for monitoring the medication's impact on your child's symptoms and any noticeable side effects. The goal is to monitor your child's physical and mental symptoms to discern if the medication is having an optimal effect on ADHD symptoms while not creating any unwanted results. The prescribing doctor may provide you with a symptom tracker that can be completed both by you and your child's teacher. This will allow you to carefully monitor all the effects of your child's medication, whether positive or negative, while also ensuring a thorough picture from multiple perspectives. Do not underestimate the value of requesting your child's input. Ask your child if they notice any positive or negative changes when they are taking the medication.

If the medication is working effectively for your child, you will begin to see a noticeable decrease in ADHD symptoms. Specific areas to look for in regards to symptom reduction include increased ability to sustain attention and focus, increased attention to detail and less impulsivity both verbally and physically.

If the medication is not working effectively, you may notice minor changes in some of the areas mentioned above, but in general you will not see significant improvement. Or you may notice your child is experiencing noticeable side effects that include loss of appetite, nausea, sleep problems, headaches or increased irritability. In this case, you will need to contact the doctor to report little reduction in symptoms and noticeable side effects.

It is crucial you are monitoring, tracking and sharing your child's symptoms and side effects with the prescribing doctor. Your doctor wants to find the right medication and dose for your child, but must rely on detailed feedback from you to understand the full picture of how your child is responding to the medication. Remember that it is equally important for you to ask your child about their perspective regarding the effects of the medication. Ask your child if they notice any changes in their body, mood, level of attention, level of activity, eating habits and/or sleep cycle. Share your child's observations with the doctor as well.

One final note about medication. As your child grows and changes, their medication may need to change with them. Medication interacts with your child's body chemistry, which will change over time. Always continue to monitor for medication effectiveness and side effects so that your child's doctor can make adjustments as needed.

Looking for more information?

https://www.webmd.com/add-adhd/adhd-medication-chart

https://www.healthychildren.org/English/health-issues/conditions/adhd/Pages/Determining-ADHD-Medication-Treatments.aspx

https://childmind.org/guide/parents-guide-to-adhd-medications/

https://kidshealth.org/en/teens/ritalin.html

Section Two Summary

As in Section One, we encourage you to take these questions and bring them to conversations with members of your child's team, including their doctor, teacher, school counselor, etc.

Questions to ask DURING the diagnosis:

1. How will the professional diagnose ADHD?

2. How likely is it that my child will be identified as having ADHD if they really don't have it?

3. Does my child have simple or complex ADHD? How will I know?

4. Are there other conditions that are likely to coexist with ADHD that I should be aware of and monitoring for?

5. What is ADD and how does it relate to ADHD?

6. What is the difference between a school evaluation and an outside evaluation?

7. What process can I expect in a school evaluation?

8. What process can I expect in a private evaluation?

9. What is an IEP and does my child need one?

10. What is a 504 plan and does my child need one? What supports does a 504 plan provide?

11. Is ADHD considered a learning disability?

12. What is executive function and what does it have to do with ADHD?

13. If my child is prescribed medication, what can I expect?

Remember, your child's best advocate is you! This information can be a lot to process, so take a breath and use these questions to continue having deeper conversations regarding your child. Do not be afraid to ask as many questions as you would like and to continue asking for clarification until you truly understand what the ADHD diagnosing process entails.

We understand the diagnosing stage can be confusing. Please feel free to reach out to Russell Coaching so we can support you.

Section Three

Asking The Right Questions

After

The Diagnosis

1. If my child doesn't have ADHD, what do I do now?

You have gone through all of the interviews, rating scales and testing only to find out your child does not have ADHD. This may bring a sense of relief at one level knowing your child does not have ADHD but increase feelings of anxiety at another level as you wonder what exactly is going on with your child.

The good news is that you have ruled one condition out. The bad news is you will need to continue to work with specialists to determine why your child is experiencing the symptoms that they are. There are numerous conditions and problems that could cause similar symptoms to ADHD. Work with your specialist to determine what the next steps are in the process of diagnosing your child's symptoms. Your next steps may include additional evaluations or referrals to another specialist. Whatever the next steps are, stay focused on your goal of getting help for your child.

Looking for more information?

https://www.webmd.com/add-adhd/childhood-adhd/medical-conditions-like-adhd

https://www.additudemag.com/the-truth-about-girls-adhd/

https://www.washingtonpost.com/health/how-women-and-girls-with-adhd-are-given-short-shrift-with-treatment-other-forms-of-help/2020/05/15/a7971486-8596-11ea-878a-86477a724bdb_story.html

2. If my child does have ADHD, what do I do now?

If your child does indeed have ADHD, now you can begin the process of establishing a multimodal treatment plan for your child. Start with the specialist who diagnosed your child. Prepare a list of questions to ask the specialist so that you thoroughly understand what ADHD is, what it is not, how ADHD is affecting your child now, how it can affect your child in the future and what the specialist recommends for a treatment plan. If you choose to do online research regarding ADHD, be sure you are using reputable sources such as The American Academy of Pediatrics (AAP), The American Academy of Child and Adolescent Psychiatry (AACAP), or credible organizations such as the national nonprofit organization, Children and Adults with Attention-Deficit/Hyperactivity Disorder (CHADD).

You may also want to consider whether or not you need a more specialized approach. If the diagnosing doctor was your child's pediatrician, you may want to seek out the services of a child psychiatrist or psychologist who specializes in ADHD treatment. It is important to remember that medication alone will not constitute your child's treatment plan. As we mentioned in Section One, the American Academy of Pediatrics recommends a multimodal approach that includes medication, parent training and education, a school plan and skills training for your child.

Looking for more information?

https://www.webmd.com/add-adhd/childhood-adhd/child-adhd-diagnosis-guide#:~:text=with%20these%20effects.-,Talk%20With%20Your%20Child's%20School,(IEP)%20for%20your%20child.

https://www.understood.org/en/articles/my-child-was-just-diagnosed-with-adhd-now-what

3. What role will the diagnosing professional play in treatment?

What role the diagnosing professional will play in your child's treatment plan depends on the specialty area of that professional. In most cases, the diagnosing professional will meet with you to provide ADHD informational materials and information about support resources available to you. You may receive a referral for courses designed to educate parents of children diagnosed with ADHD.

If your child's pediatrician is the diagnosing specialist for your child, they may refer you to a child psychologist for additional support. The diagnosing professional may recommend behavioral therapy for your child. In short, what role the diagnosing professional will play varies greatly depending on their specialty. Regardless of who the diagnosing professional is, your child's treatment plan should include a collaborative effort.

4. What should the treatment team look like for my child? What professionals should be on our team?

The African proverb, "It takes a village" is certainly applicable when it comes to your child's treatment team. Your child's treatment team will consist of a variety of individuals who are each looking through a different lens. Whatever the composition of your child's team, it should represent a holistic, collaborative approach to your child's care.

First and foremost, in comprising your child's treatment team, is you! As the parent, you are an integral component of your child's treatment team. Other essential players in your child's treatment team will include the diagnosing professional, your child's teacher(s), designated school personnel, any applicable mental health professionals, and any other specialists specific to your child's ADHD care such as speech or occupational therapists. Your child's treatment team may also include a sports or academic coach.

Looking for more information?

https://www.webmd.com/add-adhd/guide/adhd-health-care-team

https://www.additudemag.com/adhd-treatment-team/

5. What is evidence-based, scientific treatment for ADHD?

Your child's treatment plan will be based on the unique needs of your child. However, there are commonly used evidence-based, scientifically valid treatment options you should look for in a treatment plan. If your child is under 6 years of age when diagnosed with ADHD, the American Academy of Pediatrics (AAP) recommends evidence-based behavior management therapy (parent training in behavior management) as the primary method of treatment.

Parents sometimes wonder why they need specialized training. It is important to remember that your child's ADHD diagnosis does not just impact your child at school, it also impacts your child at home. ADHD can impact family relationships as well as peer relationships. Behavior therapy is designed to equip parents with behavior management training skills to strengthen and/or learn positive skills while reducing challenging behaviors. Behavior therapy can also equip teachers with behavior interventions to be used in the classroom. If your child under

6 does not show significant improvement from behavioral interventions, the Food and Drug Administration (FDA) approved medication, Methylphenidate, may be considered in addition to behavioral interventions.

If your child is over 6 years of age when diagnosed with ADHD, the AAP recommends an FDA approved medication in addition to evidence-based behavior management therapy and classroom interventions. Your child's school should be a part of their treatment plan and the plan itself should include educational interventions and modifications as well as individual educational supports. Your child's treatment plan may also include mental health treatment for your child and you as the parent. Mental health treatment can address issues such as relationship challenges, behavior concerns, and self-confidence/self-esteem deficits.

Looking for more information?

https://publications.aap.org/pediatrics/article/144/4/e20192528/81590/Clinical-Practice-Guideline-for-the-Diagnosis?autologincheck=redirected

6. Who can prescribe and manage medications?

As we discussed in earlier sections, there are numerous qualified professionals who can diagnose ADHD. However, just because a professional is qualified to diagnose ADHD does not mean they are qualified to prescribe and manage medication for ADHD. Your child's pediatrician or any other medical doctor, such as a neurologist, is qualified to prescribe medication. A child and adolescent psychiatrist can also prescribe and manage medication. A psychologist, however, is not qualified to prescribe or manage your child's medication.

Looking for more information?

https://www.verywellmind.com/add-and-treatment-how-to-find-a-doctor-for-add-20892

7. **Why are there so many different ADHD medications? Which one is best for my child?**

The fact that there are so many different FDA approved ADHD medications is a clear indicator that there is no one-size-fits-all approach to medication. The sheer number of medications approved to treat ADHD can be overwhelming itself. The primary reason there are so many different FDA approved medications to treat ADHD is related to your child's biochemical makeup. ADHD medication works with your child's body chemistry and metabolism. Every child's body chemistry and metabolism responds differently to different medications.

ADHD medications include stimulants and nonstimulants. Stimulants are generally considered the default option as the majority of children with ADHD will experience symptom reduction with stimulant medication. Approximately 80% percent of children respond well to stimulant medication. For those who do not, nonstimulant medication may be helpful. For some children, a stimulant medication may work well in general but does not entirely reduce all of their symptoms. In this case, the prescribing doctor may also prescribe a nonstimulant medication alongside the stimulant medication in an effort to alleviate all symptoms.

Looking for more information?

https://www.additudemag.com/stimulants -vs-nonstimulant-adhd-medication-video/

8. Are there over-the-counter ADHD medications my child can take?

There are no over-the-counter medications for ADHD. If you are using medication, it will be medication that is prescribed by a medical professional. There are some supplements that are marketed with the claim to help alleviate ADHD symptoms. However, there have been no long term studies to support the use of any supplements for ADHD. In addition, supplements are not regulated or monitored by the FDA and should be taken with caution.

Looking for more information?

https://www.webmd.com/add-adhd/childhood-adhd/can-you-treat-adhd-without-drugs

9. What are the short and long term side effects associated with taking or not taking ADHD medication?

As we mentioned earlier, ongoing side effects are an indication that a particular medication may not be right for your child. However, it is common for some initial side effects to occur as your child's body adjusts to the medication. It may take a few days or even weeks for the early side effects to dissipate. These common early side effects include trouble sleeping, loss of appetite, nausea and headaches. It will be important to note these side effects, as well as their intensity and duration, to share with your child's doctor. The doctor may be able to make adjustments such as changing the dose/time of the medication to help alleviate the side effects. If the side effects persist, your doctor will most likely prescribe a new medication that may work better with your child's body chemistry.

Although serious side effects are very rare, it is important to be aware of what they might include. Rare, but serious, side effects of ADHD medication can include hallucinations, suicidal thoughts, tics, heart problems or liver damage. Again, these very serious side effects are extremely rare, but if you were to observe any signs of these side effects you should not give your child another dose of the medication until you have contacted their doctor.

Stimulant medications have been studied long term in patients taking them for conditions such as narcolepsy. Research has found no major concerns in terms of long term side effects or health risks in patients with long term use of stimulant medications. Many parents find this research on long term side effects helpful when considering medication.

The other side to consider is what is likely if your child isn't treated...

Looking for more information?

https://childmind.org/article/side-effects-of-adhd-medication/

https://www.webmd.com/add-adhd/childhood-adhd/risks-of-untreated-adhd#:~:text=Children%20with%20untreated%20ADHD%20may,struggle%20to%20control%20their%20emotions.

https://www.smartkidswithld.org/getting-help/adhd/untreated-adhd-lifelong-risks/

10. When will my child be able to stop taking ADHD medication? Is it possible my child continues medication into adulthood?

It is very possible that your child continues medication into adulthood and there is nothing wrong with that scenario. As you know, there are no known serious long term side effects of ADHD medication. The end goal of ADHD treatment is to ensure your child is able to function at their best without symptoms, even if that means continuing medication into adulthood. If that is the case for your child, you can move forward with the comfort that your child has medication that is helping to control the neurological symptoms that would otherwise negatively impact their life.

There is a possibility that your child outgrows their symptoms and is able to eventually stop taking medication in their later teenage years. You may begin to notice things like your child not having symptoms after missing a few doses of their ADHD medication, or you realize you can't remember your child displaying any symptoms at all over the past year.

Even if you do notice these positive changes, you should plan to consult the prescribing doctor before making any decisions. Just like your child's body needed time to adjust to medication in the beginning and the doctor needed time to determine the right medication in the beginning; your child's body will need time to adjust to weaning off the medication and the doctor will need time to determine if doing so is effective. There was a process to determine whether or not your child had ADHD and whether or not a particular medication was beneficial to your child. There will be a similar process in reverse should you start to notice signs your child may be ready to stop taking medication.

Looking for more information?

https://www.additudemag.com/can-you-make-it-without-adhd-medication/

https://chadd.org/adhd-weekly/grow-out-of-adhd-not-likely/

https://www.webmd.com/add-adhd/childhood-adhd/news/20210818/only-1-in-10-kids-with-adhd-will-outgrow-it

11. What is parent training and education and who can conduct it?

First, know that parent training and education will not directly affect your child's symptoms. Medication is the primary intervention that will directly affect your child's symptoms. However, in addition to medication regulating the neurological part of ADHD, parent training and education helps to regulate the skills component of ADHD. Parent training (or behavioral therapy) involves the parent and child working together, therefore both parents and children learn new skills. In general, parent training and education programs cover creating structure through organization, consistent routines and clearly communicated instructions/expectations as well as using positive feedback, rewards for motivation and logical consequences. The primary goals of most parent training and education programs are to strengthen positive behaviors your child exhibits, limit negative behaviors your child exhibits through teaching a replacement skill and teaching your child how to improve their emotional communication skills.

There are several different types of parent training and education. Some of the most commonly recognized include but are not limited to: Parent-Child Interaction Therapy (PCIT), Parent Management Training (PMT). Positive Parenting Program (Triple P) and Incredible Years Parenting Program (IY). Behavioral therapy is generally conducted by clinical psychologists who are trained in the specific therapy being offered. It will be important to find a qualified and trained therapist who can provide this whole family approach type of therapy. You can ask your pediatrician or primary care physician for recommendations, your child's school for recommendations, or you can use reputable directories such as those provided by CHADD.

Looking for more information?

https://www.cdc.gov/ncbddd/adhd/behavior-therapy.html

https://chadd.org/adhd-weekly/12-behavioral-programs-for-managing-adhd/

https://www.additudemag.com/adhd-behavior-therapy-parent-training-classes/

12. What does my child need from their school and how do I get school support?

Your child's school is an essential part of their treatment plan. The school's role is to provide a psychoeducational evaluation (if requested), to provide appropriate supports and to be aware of your child's diagnosis and specific needs. Your child should have either an IEP or 504 plan from their school so that they may receive any and all necessary modifications, environmental supports and strategies designed to help them succeed at school. Your child needs teachers who are aware of and provide the specific accommodations and supports your child is entitled to. Positive behavioral classroom management is an evidence-based treatment for ADHD and should accompany behavioral therapy for parents.

Looking for more information?

https://www.cdc.gov/ncbddd/adhd/school-success.html

https://www.healthychildren.org/English/health-issues/conditions/adhd/Pages/Your-Child-At-School.aspx

https://www2.ed.gov/about/offices/list/ocr/docs/dcl-know-rights-201607-504.pdf

https://www.understood.org/en/articles/the-teacher-isnt-following-my-childs-iep-what-can-i-do

13. How can my child learn the skills they need?

Some of the skills your child needs will be learned through behavioral therapy. Behavioral therapy may focus on your child building skills such as following simple instructions, keeping their room clean, getting ready in a timely manner for school, or completing daily chores. Behavioral therapy may also focus on skills needed for school such as paying attention in class, refraining from blurting out answers and getting to class on time. Punishment rarely works for children or teens with ADHD.

Skill building will also occur through parental supports such as consistent routines broken down into achievable steps that are clearly stated in words and/or with pictures; organizational tools such as planners, whiteboards, desk organizers, and color coded folders; and appropriate rewards for motivation. School supports that can help your child learn new skills include varied teaching methods to increase interest, brain and/or movement breaks, and organization tools in the classroom. A school plan should use positive rewards and incentives, not punishments or the taking away of recess or lunch.

Looking for more information?

https://www.helpguide.org/articles/add-adhd/teaching-students-with-adhd-attention-deficit-disorder.htm

https://www.cdc.gov/ncbddd/adhd/behavior-therapy.html

https://www.mayoclinichealthsystem.org/hometown-health/speaking-of-health/helping-a-child-with-adhd-develop-social-skills

14. What is an ADHD coach and does my child need one? How do I find the right coaching service?

Another form of skill building can take place through ADHD coaching. ADHD coaching consists of a qualified coach working one on one with your child to help strengthen their executive function skills, learn how to set and achieve goals and learn how to problem solve the challenges they face due to their ADHD diagnosis. An ADHD coach can help your child develop skills such as planning skills, time management skills, organizational skills, goal-directed achievement skills, prioritization skills and problem-solving skills.

An ADHD coach is not a therapist, tutor or teacher. Rather, an ADHD coach can be thought of as comparable to a sports coach. Your child's ADHD coach will be someone on the sidelines who helps your child develop skills, achieve their goals, regroup when necessary, and encourage their progress.

Youth with ADHD ranging from late elementary school through college can benefit from ADHD coaching. Many children excel with an individualized coaching experience that targets their executive function challenges as well as strengths. If your child has their neurological symptoms properly regulated through medication yet still struggles with executive functioning skills such as planning, organization, time management, task initiation and goal-directed persistence, an ADHD coach will probably benefit your child. Additionally, from the time of middle school or puberty, your child may be much more open to getting help from a coach than from their parents.

ADHD coaching is not covered by insurance, not regulated, and not licensed. Therefore, it is important to do your research and look for a reputable company with credentialed coaching staff. Quality ADHD coaching providers utilize coaches credentialed in the fields of education, psychology and social work. In addition, a reputable coaching company will provide coaches who are experienced with and trained in working with neurodivergent students.

One final note about ADHD coaching; some students welcome the thought of having a coach and view the coaching/coachee relationship as a support to help them succeed. Many students thrive with the individualized support and individualized focus ADHD coaching can provide. However, some students can be resistant to the idea of coaching. In those cases, it will be important to hear your child's concerns and not dismiss them. Instead, help your child feel both seen and heard so they know that their perspective is valued. Once you have a better understanding of your child's perspective, you can discern what information to provide your child with that will help them feel more receptive to the idea of coaching. For some, it will help to provide information regarding success rates of other students with ADHD receiving coaching. For others, they will benefit from hearing from a peer with ADHD who has benefited from coaching. It will be useful to talk to your diagnosing professional as well as the ADHD coach on ways to help your child feel more receptive to the coaching process. Choosing a coaching service that places an emphasis on relationship building, positive feedback, and the child's strengths will be especially important for students resistant to ADHD coaching.

Looking for more information?

https://chadd.org/wp-content/uploads/2018/06/ATTN_12_13_RightForTeen.pdf

https://www.smartkidswithld.org/getting-help/adhd/adhd-coaching-can-it-work-for-your-child/

https://chadd.org/about-adhd/coaching/

15. What is and is not evidence-based, scientific treatment for ADHD?

In general, the AAP recommends FDA approved medication and behavioral therapy as the most effective, evidence-based and scientifically validated treatments for ADHD. Research in effective treatments for ADHD continues to grow and some alternatives do show promise but have not yet been researched enough to be proven effective. Methods showing some promise through initial trials include neurofeedback, working memory training, mindfulness, yoga, omega-3 supplements and exercise. However, even if approved, these methods will most likely be recommended in addition to FDA approved medication and/or behavioral therapy. If you are considering trying one of these newly researched methods, consult your child's doctor before doing so. As of now, FDA approved medication and behavioral therapy remain the most effective and only evidence-based treatments available for ADHD.

There are numerous methods

marketed as alternative ADHD treatments that are significantly less effective than traditional multimodal therapy and in some cases have no evidence for effectiveness. These include dietary restrictions, elimination diets, chiropractic care, vitamins, minerals and herbal supplements such as zinc or iron, melatonin, brain training games, and aromatherapy. While you may be able to find many people online praising these methods, remember that these methods do not have significant, strong research behind them to support claims of success. We would suggest that at minimum, if you are considering one of these unproven methods, you consult your child's doctor beforehand.

Looking for more information?

https://www.webmd.com/add-adhd/childhood-adhd/adhd-alternative-treatments

https://health.ucdavis.edu/mindinstitute/research/about-adhd/adhd-treatment.html

https://www.contemporarypediatrics.com/view/nonpharmacologic-treatments-adhd-lack-evidence-base

16. What causes ADHD? Is there something I did wrong or could have done differently to prevent my child from having ADHD?

First and foremost, it is essential to understand that scientists have not yet pinpointed an exact cause of ADHD. Extensive research devoted to determining the root cause of ADHD is ongoing. There is evidence to suggest possible risk factors that may contribute to an ADHD diagnosis. Possible risk factors include a genetic risk that results from having a blood relative, such as a parent or sibling, with ADHD; brain injury; early exposure to environmental toxins, pesticides and pollutants; low birth weight; premature birth; and maternal drug, alcohol and tobacco use during pregnancy.

There is also extensive research devoted to determining factors that do not contribute to an ADHD diagnosis. There are many common misconceptions regarding what causes an ADHD diagnosis. These include parenting styles, diet, too much screen time, poverty, stress, traumatic experiences, allergies or immunizations. However, research has shown that despite common misconceptions, these factors do not cause ADHD.

The bottom line is there is no research-proven, definitive cause of ADHD. Whatever you did or did not do as a parent cannot be changed. Ruminating or blame will not help your child manage their ADHD. Regardless of what you did or did not do in the past, the most helpful thing you can do for your child now is to educate yourself about their ADHD diagnosis, participate in behavioral training, and work collaboratively with your child's treatment team to determine the most effective medication and environmental supports to help your child be successful.

Looking for more information?

https://www.healthychildren.org/English/health-issues/conditions/adhd/Pages/Causes-of-ADHD.aspx

https://www.webmd.com/add-adhd/adhd-causes

17. How do I explain my child's diagnosis to my child, friends and family?

Understandably, many parents feel at a loss for words on how to discuss their child's ADHD diagnosis with, not only their child, but close friends and family as well. As you think through and prepare for sharing and discussing your child's diagnosis, make sure that you are fully educated yourself. Read over any literature from your doctor or training classes so that you can ensure you are using the correct vernacular. It will be important that you describe your child's ADHD in terms of something your child *experiences*, not something your child *is*.

When sharing the diagnosis with your child, be prepared to emphasize that there is nothing inherently wrong with your child. Explain that we all have brains and bodies that work a little differently and in your child's case, this is just the way their brain works. Help your child better understand by highlighting other familiar differences such as a child who sees differently and requires eye glasses. Be prepared to explain to your child a little about how their brain works differently and how things such as paying attention or sitting still might be harder for them than others. You may also want to consider age appropriate ADHD resources you can share with your child such as *A Walk in the Rain with a Brain* by Edward Hallowell or *The ADHD Workbook for Teens: Activities to Help You Gain Motivation and Confidence* by Lara Honos Webb.

When choosing to share your child's diagnosis with family and friends, it will be helpful to emphasize that ADHD is a neurological disorder, not a willpower or behavior disorder. Your family and friends may not be very educated about ADHD and consequently have many false assumptions. In addition to providing a brief understanding of what ADHD is, you may also want to consider helping others understand what kind of symptoms your child exhibits that are related to their disorder. If your child spends a significant amount of time with family members, it will be useful to provide some simple strategies that family members can use to help your child be more successful.

Looking for more information?

https://www.webmd.com/add-adhd/childhood-adhd/features/adhd-talking-to-child

https://chadd.org/adhd-weekly/talking-with-your-child-about-adhd/

https://www.additudemag.com/how-to-help-people-understand-adhd/#:~:text=Talk%20Down%20Your%20Family&text=Tell%20her%20that%20it's%20important,you%20know%20about%20the%20condition.

18. What questions should I be asking for my grade school ADHD child?

There are some questions to ask about ADHD that will be specific to your child's age and school grade. Below, you will find a sampling of those questions as they relate to a grade school child with ADHD, as well as answers you might expect to receive.

Question: *How do I learn more about ADHD in grade schoolers?*

Answer: In addition to asking the diagnosing professional for specific information regarding how ADHD will impact your child in the grade school years, you can also look for reputable resources specific to grade schoolers with ADHD such as this article published by Understood.org.

https://www.understood.org/en/artic
les/adhd-in-grade-school-4-signs-
you-might-see

Question: *Can my grade schooler benefit from ADHD coaching?*

Answer: An ADHD coach will not be beneficial until your child is in at least the 5th grade. However, parents can certainly benefit from ADHD coaching during their child's earliest years. If you have completed behavior therapy and still need additional support in helping your child, an ADHD parent coach may be a good resource for you.

Question: *How do I help my child's teachers understand ADHD?*

Answer: While it may seem like your child's teachers should be very knowledgeable about ADHD and how to help your child succeed, that is not always the case. Many teachers have little to no training about ADHD.

Your child's diagnosing clinician may provide you with resources to share with your child's teachers. In addition, you can seek out information from reputable sources such as these free "Tips for Teachers" teachers videos from CHADD. In addition, CHADD offers a fee based Teacher Training Program. If your child's school does not already provide teachers with this training program as a part of their ongoing professional development, now would be a great time to advocate for them doing so!

Question: *How often should teachers be providing feedback to a prescribing medical professional?*

Answer: For ongoing communication, your child's teacher should be providing feedback to the prescribing medical professional at least once a semester. However, if your child is just beginning the medication titration process, your child's teacher will be asked to provide feedback more often. In the beginning stages, the teacher could be providing feedback once or twice monthly.

19. What questions should I be asking for my middle schooler with ADHD?

As your child ages, there will be questions applicable that have not been applicable to your child in the past. Below, you will find a sampling of those questions as they relate to a middle school child with ADHD, as well as answers you might expect to receive.

Question: *Does my child's medication need to change now that they are getting older?*

> **Answer**: More than likely, yes. As your child ages, their brain/body chemistry changes and they may not be as responsive to their medication as they once were. In addition, your child's symptoms can change over time which may prompt the diagnosing professional to find a new medication to better address the new symptoms.

Question: *Can my middle school child benefit from ADHD coaching?*

Answer: Yes! Many middle school students have benefited from ADHD coaching. At this age, your child is developmentally ready to work with a coach so that they may set and achieve goals for skill development.

Question: *How does ADHD look in kids as they start to go through puberty? What are the interactions?*

Answer: While symptoms of ADHD in teens are similar to symptoms of ADHD in children, during the teen years ADHD symptoms may get worse. It's important to know that hormonal changes will most likely impact your child's symptoms. How the hormonal changes impact your child and their ADHD symptoms will depend on your child's gender. In boys, elevated testosterone levels may create an increase of risky behaviors. In girls, elevated estrogen and progesterone levels may create mood disorders as well as increased academic problems and aggressive behavior.

Question: *When is the best time to ask for teacher feedback on classroom symptoms?*

> **Answer**: Generally speaking, one month into the school year is the ideal time to request teacher feedback on classroom symptoms. As we mentioned before, the frequency of feedback from the teacher will depend on where your child is at in the diagnostic process. If your child has more than one teacher, it will be most beneficial to collect feedback from the teacher of the first class of your child's day as well as the teacher from the last class of the day.

Question: *Does my middle schooler's IEP/504 have to change? What do I do if school says it does?*

> **Answer**: While your middle schooler's IEP and/or 504 plan doesn't *have* to change, it will probably *need* to change. Your child's IEP and/or 504 plan needs to change as your child's educational needs, educational environment and ADHD

symptoms change. For instance, there may be accommodations that your child needed in elementary school such as movement breaks, that are no longer needed in middle school. Likewise, there may be new accommodations needed in middle school that weren't necessary in elementary school.

You are a critical member of your child's treatment team and should have input into their school plans. Be prepared to meet with the school appointed team regarding the contents of your child's school plan. If the school says your child's IEP and/or 504 plan needs to change and you do not agree with that decision, you can formally reject the plan. You also have the right to formally appeal any decisions the school makes regarding your child's IEP or 504 plan.

20. What questions should I be asking for my high schooler with ADHD?

As your child enters high school, there will be new questions to consider as it relates to your child's ADHD diagnosis. Below, you will find a sampling of those questions as they relate to a high school child with ADHD, as well as answers you might expect to receive.

Question: *Does my child's medication need to change now that they are getting older?*

> **Answer**: It is likely that your child's medication may need to change. Your child's symptoms may be different than in the past, their body chemistry may be different after going through puberty and new symptoms may manifest.

Question: *Can my high school child benefit from ADHD coaching?*

Answer: Yes! High school students can benefit from the individualized support and skill coaching an ADHD coach can provide. Many students describe an appreciation for the structure and accountability coaching provides.

Question: *When is the best time to ask for teacher feedback on classroom symptoms?*

> **Answer**: Just as in middle school, one month into the school year is the ideal time to request teacher feedback on classroom symptoms. However, remember that the frequency of feedback from your teens teacher will depend on where your teen is at in the diagnostic process. For instance, if your teen's diagnosing professional is seeking to find a new medication that better suits your teen at this new stage in their life, it may be appropriate to ask for more frequent teacher feedback. Remember that it will be most beneficial to collect feedback from the teacher of your teen's first class of their day as well as the teacher from the last class of their

day.

Question: *Does my high schooler's IEP/504 have to change? What do I do if school says it does?*

Answer: Your high schooler's IEP or 504 plan may or may not need to change. As within middle school, your teen's IEP and/or 504 plan needs to change as your teen's educational needs, educational environment and ADHD symptoms change. If your teen has an IEP, by law the school is required to review it annually. If your teen has a 504 plan, the law requires that the plan is reviewed periodically. Entering high school is a perfect time for review.

Remember, you are a critical member of your teen's treatment team and should have input into their school plan. Be prepared to meet with the school appointed team regarding the contents of your teen's school plan. If the school says your teen's IEP and/or 504 plan needs to change in ways you do not agree with, you can formally reject the proposed plan. As the parent, you also have the right to formally appeal any decisions the school makes regarding your child's IEP or 504 plan.

Question: *How do I get accommodations for my high schooler for IB, AP classes, the SAT, and the ACT? When should I worry about that?*

Answer: When your child is at the end of their 8th grade year, you should start the process of requesting accommodations for high specific activities such as AP classes/exams, the SAT and the ACT. There is a specific process for each.

In regards to Advanced Placement (AP) and International Baccalaureate (IB) classes, the school is bound by the same laws governing IDEA and ADA guidelines to provide the necessary services and/or accommodations for your child as they would in any other class. However, in order to receive accommodations for AP and IB exams, you must file a request with the College Board's Services for Students with Disabilities (SSD) office. Your students IEP and/or 504 plan will be needed to provide evidence of ongoing accommodations.

The process for SAT and ACT testing accommodations is similar. You must provide proof of the psychoeducational evaluation conducted by the school or private evaluator and documentation of the accommodations provided by the school (this will most likely be your student's IEP and/or 504 plan documents.) In addition, SAT testing accommodations require that the psychoeducational evaluation has been conducted in the last 5 years while the ACT requires evaluation within the last 3 years. For more detailed instructions of these accommodations, please refer to the College Board documentation guidelines found here.

https://accommodations.collegeboard.org/
request-accommodations/provide-
documentation/by-disability/adhd

Question: *Does my child need help with college essays?*

Answer: Before deciding this, reflect on whether or not your child has struggled with essay writing in the past. If so, then help with college essays could be beneficial. If not, then help with college essays probably isn't needed. Your child's high school may provide help to students grappling with the college essay process. If you or your teen feels such assistance would be helpful, don't hesitate to take the opportunity.

Question: *What should I know about ADHD and driving?*

Answer: Driving is a rite of passage most teens eagerly anticipate. For many parents, their teen entering the arena of licensed drivers is nerve wracking at best. For parents of teens with ADHD, the thought of their teen entering the arena of licensed drivers can be downright terrifying. And rightly so. The scary facts are, that for teenagers with ADHD, the risks associated with driving are greater.

Remember the core symptoms of ADHD we discussed earlier in the book? Impulsivity? Inattention? Distractibility? Any one of these alone is a scary symptom for any driver to have. Now, imagine a teen who struggles with all three and whose ADHD symptoms are exacerbated due to teenage hormones. The data is clear that teens with ADHD are statistically more likely to get into a car accident, receive a ticket for speeding and/or reckless driving or make careless mistakes with grave consequences for themselves as well as others.

As scary as this information may sound, it is important to be informed and proactive. Just as you have learned how to help your child develop the skills to be successful throughout the ADHD diagnosis, driving is no exception. Look for programs such as the ADHD Safe Driving Program outlined at CHADD.org or consider commercial programs offered that target ADHD safe driving. With the help of these programs, you can arm your teen with essential safety strategies.

21. What questions should I be asking before my teen with ADHD starts college?

While graduating high school was certainly a milestone moment to celebrate in your teens life, the game's not over yet. There are several questions specific to your college student with ADHD that you will want to consider. Below, you will find a sampling of those questions as they relate to a college student with ADHD, as well as answers you might expect to receive.

Question: How many students with ADHD successfully graduate from college?

> **Answer**: In the book *ADHD in adults: What the Science Says*, Barkley, Murphy and Fischer state that in a small sampling, 9.1% of hyperactive young adults diagnosed with ADHD graduated from college while 68% of young adults in the control group graduated from college. There are several studies which suggest similar data. The numbers are scary if you are the parent of a college bound child with ADHD.

Question: What predicts success in college for students with ADHD?

Answer: The good news is that there are some predictors of success for college students with ADHD. We can predict higher success if your young adult:

- Maintains consistent and appropriate use of their ADHD medication. This means taking their prescribed dose on a daily basis at the recommended time without deviation from the routine.
- Accesses and actively engages in the use of university supports such as accommodations, counseling services, writing centers, and tutoring services.
- Has ongoing accountability. You may have imagined that by the time your child was old enough for college, you wouldn't need to still check in regarding their homework, studying, grades, attendance and activities. This is not the case for your ADHD college student. They need accountability, monitoring,

ongoing communication and support. Your student needs both your watchful eye and your loving understanding.

- Schedules appropriately. This is one of many examples at which your college student may need your support and guidance. As they are planning out their college schedule, help them determine when is the best time for classes, how many classes in a day is realistic, and how much of an overall course load can they realistically manage.
- Mental Health Care. If appropriate supports are not in place, mental health quality and care tend to deteriorate. Mental health care can look like formal sessions with a therapist but also includes factors such as a regular sleep routine, regular physical exercise and predominantly healthy food choices.

Question: Does my child's medication need to change now that they are getting older?

Answer: More than likely, your child's medication needs will have changed several times over the course of their journey with ADHD. This is completely normal. For your college student, it will be important that your child sees a doctor who regularly treats college students for ADHD. Your child should regularly see their ADHD specialist and would get the most benefit from seeing their doctor once a month during the first year of college.

Question: Can my college student benefit from ADHD coaching?

Answer: Yes! Even if your student hasn't had an ADHD coach in the past, coaching can still have an impact even if begun in college. An ADHD coach provides another level of accountability and support, both of which are vital to success.

22. What are the consequences of untreated ADHD?

Untreated ADHD can have significant and often severe negative impacts on how your child performs at school in general, their grades, their behavior, their performance in sports, their performance at work and the quality of their relationships with others, including family and friends. Untreated ADHD can even impact your child's safety as research indicates that youth with untreated ADHD are more likely to get injured and require emergency room treatment. In short, untreated ADHD can have a negative impact on almost every area of your child's life.

As your child enters their teenage years, the consequences of untreated ADHD may become even more severe. As a teenager with untreated ADHD, your child is at greater risk for a car accident. In addition, the consequences of not being able to plan, organize and initiate tasks become even greater in high school than in the lower grades. Teens with untreated ADHD are more likely to self medicate with drugs or alcohol. Teens and young adults with untreated ADHD are statistically more likely to experience unwanted pregnancy as well as sexually transmitted diseases. As an adult with untreated ADHD, your adult child has a statistically higher chance of divorce and/or job loss. Adults with untreated ADHD are also more likely to experience mental health challenges.

The research is clear. There are serious consequences of untreated ADHD. Your child's ADHD is not likely to disappear on its own and consequences can worsen as the stakes get higher in high school, college and everyday life.

Looking for more information?

https://www.webmd.com/add-adhd/childhood-adhd/risks-of-untreated-adhd

https://www.healthline.com/health-news/children-who-dont-get-adhd-treatment-can-have-long-lasting-problems-into-adulthood-051215

https://www.additudemag.com/adhd-symptoms-in-teens/

23. What's with the alphabet soup? How am I supposed to make sense of all these acronyms?

There are a lot of acronyms that can be associated with the world of ADHD. Here is a list of some of the most common acronyms you might come across. Being familiar with them will help you stay afloat in the alphabet soup of the ADHD world.

AACAP (American Academy of Child and Adolescent Psychiatry)
AAP (American Academy of Pediatrics)
ACT (American College Test)
ADA (Americans with Disabilities Act)
ADDA (Attention Deficit Disorder Association)
ADHD (Attention Deficit Hyperactivity Disorder)
BRS (Behavior Rating Scale)
CD (Conduct Disorder)
CDC (Center for Disease Control)
CHADD (Children and Adults with Attention-Deficit/Hyperactivity Disorder)
DMDD (Disruptive Mood Dysregulation Disorder)
EF (Executive Function)

FDA (Food and Drug Administration)
IB (International Baccalaureate)
IDEA (Individuals with Disabilities Education Act)
IEP (Individualized Education Plan)
LD (Learning Disability)
NAMI (National Alliance on Mental Illness)
NIMH (National Institute of Mental Health)
OCD (Obsessive Compulsive Disorder)
ODD (Oppositional Defiant Disorder)
OT (Occupational Therapy)
SAT (Scholastic Aptitude Test)
SPD (Sensory Processing Disorder)
SSD (College Board's Services for Students with Disabilities)
TBI (Traumatic Brain Injury)
2e (Twice exceptional)

24. Will it get better? When do I stop worrying about my ADHD child's future?

While every parent worries about their child's future from time to time, as a parent of a child with ADHD you may have ongoing worries about your child's challenges and how they will impact your child's future.

The bad news: the beginning stages of an ADHD diagnosis can be rough on parents and on the child. First, you struggle with just coming to the understanding that your child is experiencing challenges outside of the normal developmental trajectory and you need to seek help to determine what is going on. Then, you face the ongoing appointments, rating scales, questions, and evaluations as the professionals seek to determine the correct diagnosis for your child. Once you have reached that stage, you then move into the worries that come with determining the right treatment plan for your child and the challenges of navigating the titration process. As you work through the stage of finding the right treatment plan for your child, you may feel like there will never be a light at the end of the tunnel. This is the stage where we encourage you to take a deep breath and embrace the process. It takes time to determine the right treatment plan and for that plan to begin working for your child. This stage may be quite bumpy.

The good news: it does get better! At some point, you will look back and realize all of the symptoms that once plagued your child haven't appeared in quite awhile. You'll realize that almost without you noticing, the road has gotten a little less bumpy and actually has a few smooth stretches! You'll notice your child is becoming more successful in school, in relationships and overall in life. You'll notice you can breathe a little easier and have started to worry a little less.

The "You can handle this" news: You'll probably never stop worrying about your child's future. After all, you are their parent and worrying about your child is part of the job description. There are always going to be moments when you think you've crossed a hurdle and can look forward to smooth sailing, until life throws you a curveball. And you can count on curveballs with your child's ADHD diagnosis. Remember that as your child grows and changes, how ADHD manifests in their life will change as well.

Keep your eye on the goal of doing whatever it takes to help your child successfully navigate life with an ADHD diagnosis and plan to roll with the punches as best you can. Although we know that symptoms of ADHD are likely to persist into adulthood, the good news is that effective treatment strategies (i.e., medication and use of environmental supports) are available to help adolescents and adults improve their ability to meet daily expectations. You are your child's number one supporter, fiercest advocate and the single most influential figure in their life. You can handle this!

Looking for more information?

https://www.healthyplace.com/adhd/childr
en-behavioral-issues/prognosis-for-
adhd-in-children

https://chadd.org/adhd-weekly/adhd-
changes-in-adulthood/

https://www.nationwidechildrens.org/fami
ly-resources-
education/700childrens/2018/05/adhd-as-
a-child-develops

Section Three Summary

As in Section One and Two, we encourage you to take these questions and bring them to conversations with members of your child's team, including their doctor, teacher, school counselor, etc.

Questions to ask AFTER the diagnosis:

1. If my child doesn't have ADHD, what do I do now?

2. If my child does have ADHD, what do I do now?

3. What role will the diagnosing professional play in treatment?

4. What should the treatment team look like for my child? What professionals should be on our team?

5. What is evidence-based, scientific treatment for ADHD?

6. Who can prescribe and manage medications?

7. Why are there so many different ADHD medications? Which one is best for my child?

8. Are there over-the-counter ADHD medications my child can take?

9. What are the short and long term side effects associated with ADHD medication?

10. When will my child be able to stop taking ADHD medication? Is it possible my child continues medication into adulthood?

11. What is parent training and education and who can conduct it?

12. What does my child need from their school?

13. How can my child learn the skills they need?

14. What is an ADHD coach and does my child need one? How do I find the right coaching service?

15. What is and is not evidence-based, scientific treatment for ADHD?

16. What causes ADHD? Is there something I did wrong or could have done differently to prevent my child from having ADHD?

17. How do I explain my child's diagnosis to my child, friends and family?

18. What questions should I be asking for my grade school ADHD child?

19. What questions should I be asking for my middle schooler with ADHD?

20. What questions should I be asking for my high schooler with ADHD?

21. What questions should I be asking before my teen with ADHD goes off to college?

22. What are the consequences of untreated ADHD?

23. What's with the alphabet soup? How am I supposed to make sense of all these acronyms?

24. Will it get better? When do I stop worrying about my ADHD child's future?

Remember, your child's best advocate is you! We know an ADHD diagnosis triggers a new set of questions and uncertainties. Do not be afraid to ask as many questions as you would like and to continue asking for clarification until you truly understand what an ADHD diagnosis means for your child and your family.

We understand receiving a diagnosis can be emotional. Please feel free to reach out to Russell Coaching so we can support you and your child.

Afterword

By this point, we have covered a lot of information regarding every stage of your journey with ADHD. How are you feeling? Hopefully, better informed and more prepared. We anticipate this resource will serve as both a guide and ongoing reference tool for you. Take these questions to the pediatrician, psychiatrist, school, and everyone on your team--that's why we wrote this book!

If you still have questions or feel unsure about something, start with revisiting the applicable section of the book. If you still need additional support, contact your doctor, therapist, child's school, ADHD coach or join an ADHD support group. Reputable organizations offering support include CHADD local affiliate groups, the Attention Deficit Disorder Association (ADDA) parent support group, and ADDitude forums.

In addition, you can access support groups such as ADDitude – ADHD Support Group on Facebook. Other reputable resources include the American Academy of Pediatrics, the Child Mind Institute and the Center for Disease Control.

Finally, we encourage you to reach out to Russell Coaching for Students for information about ADHD coaching, academic coaching, life coaching, group coaching, specialized tutoring, parent coaching, parent workshops and a plethora of resources including webinars, podcasts, blogs, and articles. We are here for you!

Meet the Authors

Dr. Norrine Russell, Ph.D

Dr. Norrine Russell is the founder of the Russell Coaching for Students, which uses an innovative method of coaching for complex students, including those who are 2E; have ADHD, Autism, or Anxiety; and those with learning differences. This innovative method, Connected Coaching, has proven successful for hundreds of students across the United States and Canada since 2009. Dr. Russell has been a featured guest on over 25 podcasts focusing on ADHD, including ADDitude. With twenty years of experience creating positive youth development and parenting education programs, Dr. Russell has extensive knowledge of child development, learning styles, special needs, and positive parenting philosophies. She blends this knowledge to provide students and parents with comprehensive support and the tools they need to grow and thrive. Dr. Russell has a Ph.D. from Bowling Green State University with a focus on psychology and education. Prior to starting her coaching and consulting practice, Dr. Russell worked for a variety of well-known non-profit agencies, including the YWCA of the City of New York, the Tampa Metropolitan Area Y, The Ophelia Project and Boys Initiative of Tampa Bay, and One Circle Foundation.

Heidi Condrey, M.Ed

Heidi Condrey is passionate about empowering students and educators alike. Over the past twenty-two years, Heidi has worked with students and teachers in a variety of capacities. Heidi has a wealth of experience as a classroom teacher, education manager, disabilities manager, mental health manager, teacher coach, teacher mentor, student coach and professional development provider. A state licensed teacher, Heidi holds a master's degree in education with a specialization in teacher leadership. She is a Conscious Discipline® Certified Instructor and holds several certifications related to teacher observation and feedback. Her career has centered around strengthening the field of education and the empowerment of both students and their families.

Notes

Made in the USA
Las Vegas, NV
22 February 2025